Navigating Your Soul's Journey

A Guide To Discovering Deeper Truth, Meaning, and Purpose

Cynthia Shifrin, Ph.D.

Open Mind Publications
PO Box 3095, Bellevue, Washington 98009

ISBN 978-0692507490

LLC: 2015908886

Printed in the United States of America

Published August, 2015
Revised Edition

This book is not intended as a substitute for treatment with a mental health professional. The reader should consult with a mental health professional with matters relating to his/her mental and emotional health and particularly with respect to any symptoms that may require diagnosis or mental health attention.

For Max Shifrin, my son and greatest inspiration to love from the depth of my heart and Soul.

For David Levinson, my beloved husband, who loves with sweetness, passion, and an open heart.

For Shelley Grant, my closest and lifelong friend, whose love is one of my biggest blessings.

CONTENTS

PREFACE

Embarking upon a journey of spiritual awakening requires awareness, curiosity, and openness. It also requires courage to face the inevitable challenges and unknowns along the way. It is a process that involves paying keen attention like never before and seeing with spiritual eyes beyond what is obvious. What used to appear as coincidence or randomness is suddenly understood as having synchronicity, purpose, and meaning. There is a heightened realization that we're not, nor have we ever been, alone in this journey.

Being curious about our deeper Self, about the meaning of life, about our purpose for being here, and about all those big questions that long to be answered calls for a lot of Soul searching and seeking after spiritual truth. Enlightenment is a road without an intended end. It is also a journey of starts and stops, sometimes staying in one place for a while before something new motivates us to travel farther on and deeper within.

I've thought back over my own journey of spiritual awakening and how I would have appreciated having a guidebook to assist me. I would have wanted the convenience of easy-to-access, key information contained within one book and presented with a transformational tool I could put into immediate action, such as positive affirmations. So I decided to create that book with the intention to guide others.

This guidebook contains practical wisdom and universal spiritual concepts for navigating life with greater ease and Self-empowerment. It is a compilation of much of the wisdom and knowledge I've gained on my own journey of personal and spiritual growth and from my work as a psychotherapist and as a Spiritual Response Therapist. My knowledge of spirituality, of the Soul, and of the subconscious was immensely expanded through learning Spiritual Response Therapy (SRT) from its founder, the late Rev. Robert Detzler, when he was eight-six years young.

INTRODUCTION

Those who guide others spiritually, similar to guides of all kinds, can take others only as far as they've traveled themselves. Guides must personally know the terrain being traveled well enough not merely to lead, but also to teach skills for navigating the journey. This book is meant to serve as a guide on your Soul's journey. My hope is that it gives you the confidence not to worry you'll get lost along the way. And to know that even if you take a wrong turn, as we all do from time to time, you'll be able to get back on course more easily through developing spiritual skills.

The book's three chapters each address the relationship we have with our Soul, with our Self, and with others. To clarify, the Soul is our immortal, eternal spiritual being and consciousness. The Self is who we identify as through our sense of being and belonging. There is the Freudian theory of the ego and the Buddhist view. To put it simply here, the ego can either be aligned with spiritual principles and working constructively with us, or be fear-based and unwittingly working against us. I have capitalized the first letter when referring to the Soul and to the Self to honor their importance. When I make reference to God, I am referring to Source,

Spirit, or any higher power you believe in.

This guidebook does not have to be read chronologically or used cover to cover, although doing so will help strengthen your understanding of the concepts. Some parts will be easier to assimilate now and others at a later time, depending on where you are in your growth process. You may not believe in all the information within these pages, and that's okay, too. It helps to be open. It's also a book you can pick up and put down as needed. A positive affirmation accompanies each entry to further integrate its essence. I suggest saying them in front of the mirror as often as you feel the need.

The knowledge I have accumulated and share here has been of tremendous help to me, as I hope it will be for you. This book contains wisdom from spiritual, psychological, and metaphysical perspectives gained throughout my voyage in this lifetime – one in which I will continue to learn and grow until my Soul's time in this physical body comes to an end. And when it does, my Soul will move on and continue its ascension process in another realm of existence. And so is the journey of the Soul.

"The most beautiful thing we can experience is the mysterious; it is the source of all true art and science. He to whom this emotion is a stranger, who can no longer pause to wonder and stand rapt in awe, is as good as dead: his eyes are closed."

—Albert Einstein

The Relationship We Have with Our Soul

Imagine that our physical body is a ship out at sea, with our Soul, the mind of our body, at the helm steering us throughout life. If we don't follow the navigation of our higher guidance, we can easily be hijacked by the ego and feel like a ship lost at sea.

My higher guidance moves me in the direction I need to go.

Prior to this incarnation, our Soul scripted our life by choosing what lessons to learn. Other Souls agreed to join us. Contracts, vows, and agreements that we previously formed might be played out in this life. We are experiencing what our Soul chose to assist its growth in this incarnation. When we understand this, we stop feeling like a victim and more like a producer. We look for the meaning within challenging situations and see others as players acting out our script. Our free will does the directing.

I approach
challenges as
opportunities to
learn and grow.

Everything we struggle with was previously chosen by our Soul before incarnating to assist in its ascension process. Challenging issues, individuals, and circumstances represent unfinished business from past lives. Unresolved conflict, within us and in relationship with others, is trying to teach us what the Soul chose to learn; once it does, the discord has served its purpose.

I resolve conflict in healthy and productive ways, and then let it go.

Our eternal Soul is transported within a different physical form in each lifetime, based on what will best support our chosen lessons. The energies of the challenges we face, individually or with others, we have experienced in past lives. The scenarios of those other lives and the roles we played may be different, but the carry-over energy will be the same.

I work through my issues and release their discordant energy to feel free and at peace.

We are always being watched over
and supported by the spiritual realm.
Each of us has many spiritual beings
assigned to assist us while our Soul is
in physical form. All we have to do
is ask for their assistance. Whenever
we are being guided, God and the
universe provide the compass and
the road signs for us to follow.

I trust the guidance
of my heart
and intuition.

Understanding our life from a spiritual perspective empowers us to accept everything as an opportunity for growth. We awaken more and more to a profound knowing, beyond what is familiar, comfortable, or obvious. We become increasingly aware that we are navigating our Soul's journey and of life's infinite possibilities.

Everything is in
divine order
supporting my greater
good and the greater
good of all.

Our immortal Soul knows more of what we need than our human Self. By nature, the Soul seeks experience in the service of ascending, while the Self will often resist experience out of fear of the unknown. Resistance creates more suffering when painful suppressed emotions are not acknowledged, identified, and worked through.

I replace fear and resistance with courage and an openness to change in ways that serve me best.

Once our Soul awakens to its true potential, there is no going back to buying into illusions. There is no more compromising at the risk of shutting ourselves down. Being stuck in Self-doubt and only daring to dream is replaced with positive action and a fearless determination to actualize what calls to us. Our deepest longing is on fire to be fully expressed, knowing that our happiness and inner freedom depend on it.

I have everything inside of me to actualize my fullest potential.

When we awaken spirituality with an increased connection to God, we look at life beyond what is obvious. Our acknowledgment of being a spiritual being and an embodiment of God's radiant love and light expands our vision, enabling us to see life's bigger picture. We arrive at a place of knowing, without doubt, that the universe is working for and not against us.

I am a spiritual being who is supported by God and the universe in all the ways I need.

Inner peace, happiness, and freedom come from fully expressing our authenticity and releasing negative energy. It's where we honor our truth from the deepest place of who we are without allowing fear, shame, or guilt to stop us. Pain, on any level of our being, is often experienced when the Self abandons and betrays the Soul by suppressing what longs to be expressed.

I honor my true Self by expressing my authenticity to the depth of my Soul.

When we are ready and willing to follow our heart by choosing to express our Soul's deepest desires, we become fueled with such passion that we break up with old excuses why we can't do something and fall in love with all the reasons why we can.

The universe supports me in the ways and at the time I need to follow my passion.

The first step to manifesting the calling of our Soul is to focus on how we want to feel and not on the form we think it should take. Our job is to call forth those positive inner feelings and then allow the universe to do its job by guiding us to their form. Oftentimes, what we are ultimately led to is even better than we originally imagined, because God's plan for us is bigger and brighter than our own.

I align with all the
ways I want to feel,
so that the universe
can then guide me to
their correct form.

When we embrace our spiritual
beingness, we begin to dance
with our Soul's desires. We move
more instinctively to the rhythm of
God's love with every step we take.
Other kindred Souls who dance the
same dance will be drawn to partner-
ing with us, supporting us as we
support them.

I honor the divine
being in my Self
and in others.

If we're not passionate about the path we're on, in any area of our life, that's an indication it's not the right path for us. Passion is the high-octane fuel that energizes the Soul. Without it, we experience what we don't want in order to better realize what we do want.

I follow the guidance of my heart, as passion inspires me on my true path.

The Relationship We Have with Our Self

The most important relationship we have, besides with God, is with our Self. It takes honest Soul searching to identify where we're not being compassionate, kind, and forgiving to our Self. Until we learn Self love, we will continue to attract people and situations that reflect back what we need to heal within.

I love my Self in healthy ways that honor the divine being that I am.

Prayer and meditation are universal spiritual practices that connect us more directly with God and our higher guidance. Through prayer we express gratitude for our blessings, and then ask for assistance with whatever will strengthen us. Through meditation we listen for the answers intended to guide us, being given in the form of deeper awareness and greater insight.

Through prayer and meditation I express and receive communication with God and my higher guidance.

No matter what challenges and hardships we're facing, there is always something to be grateful for. Gratitude is a divine gift that has the power to move us into the present moment and instantly transmutes negative energy into positive.

I am mindful of and deeply grateful for all my blessings.

We need to be patient during our growth process. It's like making soup. Adding all the right ingredients to the pot doesn't automatically create soup. Everything has to cook and blend over time before it transforms. Even then, we have to adjust the seasoning to achieve the exact taste we want.

I am patient and trusting of my process, allowing it to come together in its perfect way and time.

What we say after the two words "I am" are some of the most powerful words we'll ever say for manifesting. The thoughts and feelings we have and the statements we express have energy, and all energy, whether positive or negative, has creative power. Our thoughts affect how we feel, and how we feel affects how we act. Be kind, compassionate, and patient when talking about your Self.

I am everything
positive.

Oftentimes attaining our goal, in any area of our life, doesn't happen as quickly or in the ways we want. There might be other important pieces, people, and paths yet to come that are necessary before meeting our goal. We need to trust in our process and know that the wisdom of the universe is much greater than our own.

I let go of fear, worry, and doubt and replace them with faith, optimism, and confidence.

When we shift into understanding life from a more spiritual perspective, we stop judging things as good or bad. We instead look for truth based on spiritual principles and universal laws, mindful of the consequences of veering from them. We are all spiritual beings, learning and growing through our human experience.

I honor the truth that
is aligned with
spiritual principles
and universal laws.

Love, in all its forms, is the most powerful positive energy there is. Giving and receiving love with an open, receptive, and responsive heart is the highest vibration of positive expression.

I am loved; I am loving; I am lovable; I am love.

We shouldn't be alarmed if it feels like we're slipping backward after moving forward, similar to how the trapeze artist must move backward in order to gain momentum to move even farther forward.

I allow myself to
move in the ways
I need with faith,
patience, and
optimism.

Our subconscious is much stronger than our conscious mind, which is why willpower often fails. Like a computer, our subconscious automatically records our perceptions of everything that is experienced through our five senses. The negative programming of false beliefs is what creates most of our suffering, as it attracts the same energy it emits, based on universal law.

I have the power to reprogram my beliefs by replacing them with positive ones.

Fear is similar to a heavy fog in how it blocks what's behind it, creating illusions to reality. As we build stronger spiritual muscles, we seek the truth that is hidden behind the illusion. Moving through the obstacle of fear allows us to see what's real and what's not.

I let go of fear to see
everything positive
that frees and
empowers me.

The importance of building strong spiritual muscles is similar to the importance of building a strong ship. Just as the weather on the sea can't be controlled, neither can we control what fate puts across our path. Strong spiritual muscles give us the inner strength to navigate tough challenges, just as a strong ship weathers rough storms. Our spirituality keeps us afloat with faith and optimism instead of sinking from fear and worry.

I have faith that everything is in divine order to support and guide me.

When we find our Self slipping into regret and shame over the past or fear and worry about the future, we need to stop and count all the things we have to be grateful for. Redirecting our focus in that way brings us back into the moment with an awareness of what really matters. Being moved back into the present is one of the best gifts of gratitude.

Expressing my gratitude keeps me in the moment with a profound awareness of how blessed I am.

While we don't have control over what fate puts across our path, we do have free will in choosing our attitude and approach toward it. Our free will is what we use to create our destiny. We can choose to feel either victimized or empowered by how we react or respond.

My positive thoughts, feelings, and actions empower me in constructive ways.

Once we overcome a hardship, heal a heartache, or transcend a trauma, what we learn throughout the process transforms us and our view of life. We are forever changed in stronger and wiser ways. Transformation expands our consciousness as we trust our spiritual senses to see, hear, and feel.

My strength,
resiliency, and
wisdom empower me.

The greater Self-knowledge and deeper awareness we gain from the lessons we learn never leave us. We may slip back into old, unhealthy patterns, but we can't stop knowing what we know we know. Sometimes slipping backward is meant to increase our awareness and deepen our insight, catapulting us farther ahead.

I do my best to learn and grow in ways that support my greater good.

Health and well-being must honor the wisdom of the mind-body-spirit connection through truth and balance. Illness is one way the physical body expresses what the emotional, mental, and spiritual bodies cannot. From a spiritual perspective, illness of any kind, on any level, can be a powerful learning partner.

I am attuned to what my body is trying to tell me on all levels of my being.

We can't allow the pain of our past to prevent us from creating the life we want now. Whatever hurtful feelings and limiting beliefs are still holding us hostage, we have the power to free our Self. The painful story we're still identifying with keeps us stuck. Whatever happened is over and done; whatever remains is to be learned from, in order to let it go.

Learning from the pain
in my past enables
me to let it go and
move forward in
healthy ways.

Change can be hard, but so is being stuck in misery. Finding happiness and fulfillment requires honesty and action. Having the courage to face the truth of what's at the root of our unhappiness begins and ends with us. Until we're completely real with our Self, we won't know what action to take.

My willingness to change and honor my true Self brings me happiness, freedom, and fulfillment.

All our challenges, especially the toughest ones, are for our growth. Perceive them as opportunities and not as punishment. When we learn what they came to teach us, we will eventually see them as contributing to our success. If we believe they are being done to us and are something to fight and fear, we are doomed to feel victimized.

My challenges come
with gifts in the
form of lessons to
learn that empower me.

No matter where we are in our life, we're good enough. We have everything we need within us, even though it may be buried underneath the debris of others' judgment and criticism. Freedom is available when we understand how others have projected their feelings of shame and unworthiness onto us, and how we unconsciously identified with those feelings.

I reclaim everything positive that I am and let go of what doesn't belong to me and never did.

Life is full of beginnings and endings. One of life's biggest challenges is to accept its inevitable uncertainty with faith and optimism. When we begin to understand that endings are actually creating space for new beginnings, we feel the support of the universe moving us toward what will serve our greater good.

I let go of endings,
as I am moved toward
new beginnings with
faith and optimism.

When it feels like we're being rejected in any way, it's actually a spiritual intervention. Once we understand we are working in partnership with God and the universe, we recover more quickly from disappointment, knowing there is another plan for us. Faith and confidence then replace worry and Self-doubt. Our punishing, fear-based ego will tell us we're not good enough, until our Soul reminds us we deserve better.

I want only what will
serve my greater good
and trust I am being
guided toward it.

Believing is the necessary first step to manifesting our fullest potential. If we don't believe in the possibility, believe in our Self, or believe in our worthiness, our limiting beliefs will create obstacles.

I believe in my
ability and
worthiness to manifest
my fullest potential.

Situational depression can be a symptom of a spiritual crisis, as the Soul struggles to align with its denied, lost, and unexpressed parts. It can also be a symptom of an existential crisis, as the Soul struggles to find its true path and purpose. What can feel to the Self like being in the throes of a breakdown can actually be a breakthrough trying to birth itself. And the labor of that birthing process can be challenging to greater or lesser degrees.

Being in full Self-expression with authenticity brings me happiness, freedom, and fulfillment.

We get used to reacting with automatic response patterns, even though we've outgrown them. As we evolve, we learn to use the positive, not yet fully expressed aspects of our Self. We have the power to recreate who we are by replacing old, out-dated parts that no longer represent our best Self. Like anything new, it may feel awkward at first, but with practice the upgraded and updated parts of us will become integrated and automatic.

I choose to be only
the best of me.

The struggles we experience are repeats from the past, calling to be resolved. They may show up in different ways, but the theme will be the same. Things that weren't fully dealt with at the time they occurred, or that we've avoided facing, are all unfinished business. When we do the internal work and replace negative beliefs with positive ones, our external life will reflect the change.

I take responsibility
for creating my
happiness and
health on all levels
of my being.

Surrender isn't about throwing in the towel when faced with hardship. It is the ability to accept what we can't change while changing what we can. Hardships test our faith and challenge our optimism as life unfolds in ways that are different than we wanted or expected. It is the divine light and love within us that replaces hopelessness with faith.

I am empowered in all
situations with
acceptance, faith, and
optimism.

It is important to release anger on all levels for our overall health and well-being. Self-forgiveness is an essential part of that process. It requires having compassion for our Self to under-stand that if we knew then what we know now, our decisions and responses would have been different.

Releasing anger and replacing it with forgiveness enables me to move forward in healthy ways.

Forgiveness of Self and others is for the purpose of releasing negative energy. To not forgive keeps us stuck in bitterness, regret, and anger. Self-punishment is when we hold on to any negative energy with our thoughts, feelings, and actions. Forgiveness is a gift we give our Self for our own health and well-being.

I forgive my Self
and others to be free
of negative energy.

If we didn't receive the kind of love we needed and wanted from a parent, it wasn't because we were unlovable. Not being given healthy love means the adults in charge of loving and nurturing us didn't have it within themselves to know how to give, not even to themselves.

I am lovable and share my love with others who have the capacity to love me in healthy ways.

The Relationship We Have with Others

It takes courage to be open and willing to share our vulnerability with an intimate partner. It's an act of trust to allow another to see the most tender parts of our heart. We have to know our Self well enough to share our truth with all its fragility. Emotional intimacy deepens love, increases desire, and strengthens connectedness.

I have the courage
and willingness
to share my
vulnerability with
my partner for greater
emotional intimacy.

Trust is an essential requirement for having a healthy relationship. Just because someone says they love us doesn't mean they know what real love is. The hurtful, disappointing, and frustrating ways others may treat us is often a direct reflection of how they were treated. Until people are willing to take responsibility for owning and healing the hurt within themselves, we can't fully trust them with our heart. Trust is earned through consistent thoughtful behavior over time.

I make wise choices
of whom to trust
with my heart.

Staying intimately and romantically involved with someone who is not returning the same feelings, for whatever reason, is a message trying to get our attention. It is triggering something within us that needs to be healed. It requires honesty to become fully aware of our Self-destructive and Self-sabotaging patterns with intimate partners to avoid repeating them.

My Self-awareness,
Self-love, and
Self-worth
strengthens my good
judgment of others.

As we grow, we ultimately outgrow our comfort zone. Anything that no longer fits us will need to be altered. Our previous ways of relating will change as well. Others we interact with may not be comfortable with our growth because it will inevitably change the dynamic of a relationship.

I stay true to my
Self with choices
that honor my growth.

No one can save anyone but themselves. It is a difficult decision to stop trying to rescue someone we love. We do so in the service of their growth and our own well-being. If we are sacrificing our health and happiness for another through rescuing, the best we can do is to bless and release them to find their own way.

I encourage and allow others to be responsible for their own life.

We teach others how to treat us by the behavior we allow. We can't assume our personal or professional partners always know what we need or want. It is our responsibility to be a strong and supportive advocate for our Self by clearly expressing what does and does not work for us.

I am clear and direct
in communicating to
others what I need
and expect.

It is a misconception that being with our Soul mate guarantees romance and harmony, even though those relationships can be very romantic and harmonious; but that's not their main purpose. Soul mates have a close connectedness that is meant to assist each other in their growth process. This isn't always easy work. Our parents, family, and friends can be our Soul mates as much as intimate partners can be.

I choose to grow with those I'm strongly connected to through kindness, respect, and patience.

When we're single and wanting to find the person meant to be ours, we need to trust that everything is in divine order to guide us to each other. The healthy love our heart longs for is a love we have to first get ready for. It is earned by healing our heart and loving our Self.

I express and receive
the healthy love
I embody.

Those that don't do what's needed to heal their inner suffering may be more invested in enduring pain than in enjoying pleasure. Ultimately, the choice to change is theirs and only theirs. If their behavior is impacting our life in negative ways, we must decide what we're willing to tolerate. It requires setting limits to protect the energy of our boundaries for our health and well-being.

I take good care of my health and well-being with strong boundaries.

There are those who partner with another out of fear of being alone, even it means compromising on being in love. And there are others who never stop searching for a magical, in-love feeling, even it means never fully committing. Some are afraid of feeling too much and others are afraid of not feeling enough. Real love can touch our heart in undeniably profound ways. And when it does, that's the magic right there, without anything to fear.

My heart is open,
receptive, and
responsive to sharing
love with another.

Those that hurt us are hurting within themselves; it has everything to do with them and not us. The experience of being on the receiving end of another's projected inner pain presents us with an opportunity to be in our higher Self by how we choose to respond.

I have compassion,
patience, and
forgiveness for
those who are unable
to manage their
inner pain.

Being romantically involved with someone who thinks they know what they want, but in fact is confused, can feel like being a front-seat passenger with the driver riding the brake. Inconsistent behavior expresses ambivalence and prevents the relationship from moving forward to the next level.

I only become seriously involved with someone who knows what they want, knows they want it with me, and is able to act on it.

When we're single and wary of getting hurt again, we have to be careful not to allow fear to put a wall around our heart. A blocked-off heart will keep out not only hurt, but love as well. Healthy love requires preparation by first working on the relationship we have with our Self. Doing so will deepen our Self-awareness of the patterns and pitfalls that have led us back to being hurt. Then one day, when we least expect it, another heart will recognize the love within ours and celebrate having finally found us.

The love, respect, and worthiness I have for my Self attracts healthy love.

Before we blame our partner for our unhappiness, we need to do some honest Soul searching. We might find it has much more to do with not having a more authentic relationship with our Self. Blaming others for our unhappiness is a way to avoid looking deeper within. Unhappiness often results from suppressing the full expression of our authentic Self.

I am the one
responsible for
creating my
happiness and
fulfillment.

Being able to truly compromise demonstrates the ability to be flexible instead of rigid. Flexibility allows us to bend without breaking when the wind blows in a new direction. It is important to make sure we're not compromising in ways that shut us down in order to please another. Compromise should result in a win-win for both; otherwise, it's about control and manipulation.

I am able to
compromise by meeting
another's needs
and my own at the
same time.

Communication at its highest level effectively arrives at mutual understanding; it's not just about expressing personal wants, needs, and opinions, although that's part of it. Without mutual understanding, communication is just talk. There is an art to asking the right questions and giving the right answers to facilitate this process. It requires quiet, contemplative listening to the other without judgment and giving up the need to be right.

My ability to express
my Self and quietly
listen to the other
without judgment
strengthens our
communication
through mutual
understanding.

Healthy love in its essence is being seen, understood, and appreciated for our authentic Self. Healthy love feels safe and even a bit scary, but in all the good ways. It's the experience of feeling we're loved for all of who we are, even when we're not our best. Real love is not inconsistent, doesn't leave us hurting, and isn't confusing. It isn't perfect; it's just perfect for us.

I give and receive healthy love that honors authenticity and full Self-expression.

Rarely do we have full awareness of the inner pain some are trying to manage and often keep hidden inside. Sometimes they will minimize their suffering and act as if they have everything handled, when they are actually overwhelmed trying to cope with their painful emotions and fearful thoughts. Be mindful not to pass judgment on others who are struggling. And remember, we're all in this together.

I see others through
kind and
compassionate eyes
without judgment.

EPILOGUE

My hope is that the information I have shared within these pages will be of valuable assistance as you move forward on your journey. Each of us is meant to discover our own deeper truth, meaning, and purpose. When we step off course from the truth of who we are to please another or to earn love and admiration, we ultimately run the risk of sacrificing our happiness in the process. The most important goal in life is to be our true Self as we express our Soul's uniqueness and spiritual essence. When we experience life fully aware and engaged, we are on the right path that will lead us to happiness that must first come from within. The things we are doing and striving for serve to align us with the truth of who we are from a heart level. The key to remember is that it is more about being than about doing. The Soul seeks to express and receive love, joy, and freedom in all forms. The fear-based ego will try to hold us back with negative thoughts and beliefs. Don't listen to its limiting voice. Instead, follow the guidance of your Higher Self, which will inform, encourage, and support you to fully embrace life and all its beautiful mystery with an open heart and an open mind. When you do, it will be the most exciting and awesome ride you will ever take.

Many blessings on your Soul's extraordinary journey.

ACKNOWLEDGMENTS

If it weren't for all the smart, innovative, and enlightened teachers and authors who have taught me about psychology, spirituality, and metaphysics, I would not have been able to write this book.

I owe the deepest gratitude to the late Rev. Robert Detzler, the founder of Spiritual Response Therapy, and to the Spiritual Response Association and its supportive community.

I want to also express my gratitude to my incredible mentor and teacher, Kathryn Hamilton-Cook, for furthering my knowledge as a Spiritual Response Therapist. My profound appreciation extends to her and to Barbara Standiford for developing Healing the Multi-Dimensional Self, which has taken my energy clearing work to a whole other level.

My heartfelt thanks go to Marie-Rose Phan-Lê for her tremendous support and validation of my work and for introducing me to the amazing Eileen Duhne, whom I want to thank from the bottom of my heart for guiding me in the development of this book to its completion.

I want to thank Mary Carman Barbosa for her wonderful assistance in editing.

I also want to thank Allen Crider for doing such a great job executing my vision for the page and cover design of this book.

I wish to thank all my clients, from the very beginning to the present, who have trusted me to guide them on their journey of personal and spiritual growth. It's been an honor to work with each of you.

Thank you also to my brother, Gary Glazer, my wonderful family, and my cherished friends, whose love and encouragement has given me the courage to put these words on paper.

With my love and appreciation,
Cynthia

ABOUT THE AUTHOR

Cynthia Shifrin, Ph.D. has over twenty-five years' experience as a psychotherapist trained in clinical psychology. Her work with clients has always honored the wisdom of the mind-body-spirit connection. The psycho-spiritual approach she uses for navigating life's challenges with an ultimate outcome of mastery, growth, and healing has been very effective for developing a stronger sense of Self and a deeper, more meaningful understanding of life. As a Spiritual Response Therapist, Cynthia works in partnership with higher guidance to identify and clear obstacles of discordant energy contained in the Soul and subconscious with clarity, precision, and integrity.

Cynthia lives in Seattle, Washington with her husband and dog. Together they have a blended family of five children and five grandchildren.

To learn more about Cynthia and her work, please visit www.cynthiashifrin.com